Mario Mantese – Master M

The Art of Not Being

Mario Mantese – Master M

The Art of Not Being

Translated from the German by Mark Doyu Albin
Edited by Doris Hüffer-Schott
Typesetting and Cover design by Marion Musenbichler
Photograph Mario Mantese © by Günther Ciupka

Original Title: Die Kunst des Nicht-Seins
© 2010 Mario Mantese, first published
by Drei Eichen Verlag, D-97762 Hammelburg

Bibliographical Information of the German National Library
This publication is listed in the German National Bibliography of the
German National Library; detailed bibliographical information
can be accessed under http://dnb.d-nb.de

ISBN 978-3-7412-3432-3

© 2016 by Mario Mantese
www.mariomantese.com

First Edition in English
Herstellung und Verlag: BoD – Books on Demand, Norderstedt

1.

Between the stillness of the forest and the silence beyond the stillness is the delicate, fluid passageway where earthly stillness enters into supernatural silence.

Where the crude force of the world ends and endless tenderness begins; here all thoughts fade away.

The awakening one discovers that his true presence began there, where he ceased to exist. Deep peace settles within, when the thinking ego vanishes. It was never more than an illusory layer of mist.

Even the sound of a leaf breaking from a twig has never disturbed the Great Silence. Perfect silence envelopes all of nature in deep serenity. Perfect silence is the nature of the awakening one.

The awakening one listens deeply into the depths of being, and is overwhelmed by the incredible beauty of abundant Spirit.

This immeasurable beauty knows nothing of its beauty, nothing of the light-filled compassion which abides in the Spirit, for there is neither one who knows nor something known.

The bright heart of the awakening one testifies to this supra-personal compassion and beauty without being aware of it, for it is free of any dichotomy or polarity!

Awareness of the consciousness which resides in the body leads beyond the word 'consciousness' and into that which was, before the body was born.

2.

The heart of the awakening one rests in the Great Silence; yes, it is the Great Silence itself.

Out of this silence flows care-free being, beauty and delight.

Through a sovereign, commanding ray shining brightly from the awakening one's heart, souls are gently elevated and integrated into ever-presence. They return to that which they always were, back into the 'all-soul,' where no separation exists.

This divine ray shines brighter than a thousand suns, and yet is hidden from human eyes. It is infinitely powerful and penetrates all inner depths and inner worlds. It opens closed hearts, closes old internal chasms, and dissolves all things past and future.

The presence of silence resembles the brilliant glow of a precious sparkling gem. The awakening being, silence itself, expresses the adornment of the Spirit.

See this clearly: the silence that is perceptible to the senses is only a sensory perception of the absence of worldly sound. The sound of thought and the sound of controlled non-thinking belong to earthly stillness, while the

Great Silence is beyond earthly stillness. That which is recognized without understanding may be called the Great Silence. The Great Silence never changes, for it is not a thing and not an object. Do not observe the intellectual mind and its activities; be aware of the silence behind it.

The charming gown of nature is only a shadow standing *before* the abundance of Spirit. The living form cannot come into existence through its own power, for it is, in reality, hollow and empty. The life-granting power, the light *behind* the shadow, is the source of all vitality.

3.

The Great Silence is not disturbed by the chirping of the small cricket. The sweet mating call which intently urges earthly creatures to union is embedded in all living beings. This small glowing flame contains nature's compelling mandate to couple, and serves to preserve the species.

In rose-tinted dream-states and pulsating infatuation, humans and animals alike are swayed into mayhem. Along their paths towards the ultimate act of pleasure humans and animals are remarkably purposeful and creative.

Those in love swim in a stormy sea of hormones and play out the roles of their lives. Whether it is the cricket or the human being, the mating desire has the same color, the same sound.

Roving ambitions are restless, but when these tenacious struggles gradually weaken, the human being is engulfed by a deep silence. Free from greed, one is transformed, and experiences beauty, joy, and contentment. The awakening one is free from identification with the body and lives detached from earthly pains and pleasures.

4.

Celestial powers breed serenity; nature's powers generate turbulence. Nature's powers are like shadows cast over celestial powers. The awakening one who avails himself completely to celestial powers realizes Totality, which is free of adversity.

Sound and the soundless are like two voices ringing out in the shadowy world of 'I'. The divine mystery of eternal presence is entirely beyond the known, beyond the 'I''s ordered and organized life, beyond all dualities.

The fervor to move forward through life carves the All-One into countless pieces. Therefore, abide within, restless one, and let what is fragmented flow back together and unify once more. The repose of non-doing is in accord with the Great Silence.

The growth of all that is transitory takes place outside of the Great Silence. Indeed, the animated and the fated never touch the Great Silence. The ephemeral does not know the enduring. Shadow knows nothing of light!

5.

To leave the body behind is like casting off an old dream. The dream was never an effigy of the Eternal, for what is breakable and ephemeral doesn't know the Eternal, and never touches what is unborn and formless.

The shadowed, bulky substance of the broad universe never originated in the Great Silence; the formed never had any share of the Formless and the known never had any share of the Unknowable.

In the awakening one, the ever-extending horizons of the personal, projected being flow back into the Great Silence, into non-being. The time of estrangement comes to an end. The overlying skins die, but the awakening one is untouched by this, for he has realized that which never dies. Nothing ever turned into anything else; silence never turned into sound.

Investigation, the search for answers, brought no peace. Absorption in delusion brought only suffering. Awakening means to see completely see through what produces suffering and delusion. This awareness is the way out of the labyrinth of the 'I'.

The Untouchable was never touched, and the Unmoving has never moved. Silence is the home of the awakening one.

No activity within – that is the Great Silence, the all-encompassing, ever-present divine power within the universe. The awakening one lives in the world without ever touching it.

6.

The affirmation of the earthly corresponds to the needs of the earthly. Through these subjective affirmations, a fictitious inner synchronization of the unreal with the unreal in the unreal, is produced.

That which manifests and is transitory is sensed as real and having true existence, although this subjective assumption, this sense, is nothing but a delusion, nothing but a manifestation in consciousness.

The luminous depths of the Great Silence endure, eternally untouched by what is finite and untrue.

Immersed in deep peace is the one who dares to jump out of the finite and into the Infinite, out of time and into the Timeless, out of space and into the Space-less. The one who goes beyond his own boundaries and looks back beholds the primal forces of light and darkness, of heaven and earth. He sees them as an old dream that the dreamer dreamed once upon a time.

When one who crosses over his own boundaries looks *ahead,* he sees *nothing.* He drowns in the boundless, nameless ocean.

The oceanic Here-and-Now-being is singular, because he knows no duality.

Free of desire, free of quarrels, dwelling in companionless silence: this is the inner life of the awakening one in Here-and-Now.

The outer margin where one was born was never more than a fleeting dream woven into the fabric of the empty world. Awakening dissolves the confusion of the old fabric and deactivates the fleeting. The world is perceived because of duality; the awakening one, on the contrary, is prior to duality.

7.

To attain stillness is not immediate. The Great Silence is. To attain stillness shuts out the Great Silence, because it firmly installs the one who is being still into the senses as a feeling and image of silence.

Attaining stillness is a controlled calming of the active senses. The one who becomes still or is still takes hold of a space within time and imagines he has touched the Unfathomable, the Great Silence.

But the vain, strident efforts of the ego follow the road of time, and confusion and death lurk along the wayside.

Intentions lead into the 'I' of the world, for the 'I' is nothing other than the relative world itself. Through the intentions of the 'I' the world appears and through the intentions of the 'I' they are preserved. The desire to do creates joy and suffering; non-doing expresses the splendor of silence.

The one who intends to become still stares into life, while the one without intention immerses himself there where evaluations have no value and all striving ends. The standpoint from which evaluations and measurements arise is seen through and dissolved by the awakening one.

Heaven and earth are no bigger than the seed of a cherry, and no thicker than a sheet of paper. How big or how small a thing appears is defined and determined by the relative viewpoint of the observing 'I'.

How real is the observer? The answer is clear for the awakening one. The observer is nothing more than a reflection in consciousness.

8.

The smile of the awakening one alights from the divine source, a mystical depth without beginning. It is a smile that has broken out of the tombs that previously concealed it. It has seen through and ended the ancient games of the 'I'.

In this smile the background upon which the human form appears has transformed into formlessness. The path of life one followed once upon a time was nothing more than a parable, an imaginary portrayal of an imageless reality.

The awakening one is aware that a letting go or dissolution of the unreal never took place; nothing ever changed from unreal to real. In the Great Silence, nothing was ever active; nothing has ever happened.

To see through the grandiose nothingness of relative external existence awakens the sunlit radiance of the heart. Now, that which was never something and never nothing awakens in flourishing hearts. The coercive spell, which tied the soul to the trials of time like a heavy ball and chain, was broken. It was cast off when the last useless words were spoken and their echo faded away, finally unheard.

The loving heart is wordless silence, the mystery exposed. The radiant luster of the Spirit shines brighter than a host of suns and never casts a shadow. This is the essence of the awakening one; he is the essential behind the inessential.

The awakening one has shaken off the foolhardy forces of the will and left authority and the desire to control behind him.

Identity and identifying lead to a downfall, a plummeting into the unconscious things of the world, into devastating heartlessness and stifling states of suffering. Consequently, the 'I' promotes as truth what is transitory and subject to death, and illusion is assumed to be something existing and real.

The vagueness and uncertainty which reside in the pleasures of the earth are set up as the criterion of daily life. Alas, the accumulation of pleasures only produces an accumulation of more desires. With such an ambiguous and disoriented life, the superb transcendence, the illumination within, is buried and suffocated.

9.

The dramaturgy of the world, where human beings have trapped themselves in three dimensions, appears to exist like a bubble floating atop a gigantic sea of energy. The sea of energy never increases or decreases, never gains or loses anything. It is as it is.

The appearance and disappearance of worldly existence takes place within this sea of energy. But the Great Silence always remains unaffected by movements and processes.

The awakening one is aware that everything which appears and flows back to the origin is that which he *never* was. What surfaces and sinks was never more than a short blink of an eye, a moment in the cosmos which never really happened.

Within his cosmic energy-consciousness the human being senses itself floating on the surface of the sea of energy, and imagines itself as something definite, as something special, as an individual. Then one awakens. Then one is aware that, in reality, one was never something or someone. The illusory 'I' has sunk to the bottom, and nothing ever comes to the surface again.

This internal retreat, the great clarification, is completed through the actual awakening from *nothingness* – though awakening is not something that happens at some particular time in some particular manner. The dissolution of the conceptual mind takes place when everything individual and illusory has finally vanished in the universal sea of energy. Hazy hallucinations are lifted when the eye is directed within.

The human being is never nothing and never everything. No, he is like a wave on the inconceivable, unknowable ocean, an echo from toneless depths.

The secret of the limitless spiritual ocean lies in the primal source of all powers which underlie the whole of existence. The apparent birth of the Spirit in the corporeal allows what exists as unity to appear as variety, but all images exist only as a reflection within the *one consciousness.*

The awakening one is aware that that which a human being calls 'the world' exists only as a perception.

Through the subjectively sensed perception an erroneous identification with what is perceived takes place. The intellectual mind which processes information traps itself in polarities which, in reality, do not exist and never did exist, because the objective world is nothing but an unreal appearance in consciousness.

Spirit is and remains eternal and unborn, free from all the restrictions of divergences. Divergences within nature exist solely as interpretations of the intellect.

Through sensory-bound differentiation one attempts to limit the Unlimited to the transitory, and confines it to observable, outwardly projected processes and events. What is identified is the transitory, that which dies. But embedded within these overlapping misunderstandings is the key to wisdom: namely, the possibility to awaken from these misunderstandings and delusions.

The most conspicuous thing about the world is that it really doesn't exist. If a human being really realizes this, he does no more harm within the world. Happy is he who has left all dull ignorance and egocentric desires behind, and overcomes the quarantine of life and death.

Awareness leads into silence. Silence is boundless and unknowable; otherwise it is not the Great Silence. One who integrates with the Great Silence is Self-realized.

What religions postulate as God's kingdom is no realm of kings; it is splendid non-existence, the home of true silence.

10.

The formed builds the vessel of the Spirit, through which its magnificence emanates. But the outer, the formed, is only the periphery of the Spirit, and not the Spirit itself.

When a human being only sees the periphery and has forgotten what lies beyond the borders of the periphery, he is driven by fear and anxiety, and worries continually about his existential needs and his future.

Like the arms of a polyp, the personified clings tightly to things and objects in the world. With this clinging a person gives things and objects meaning and importance.

These formed and condensed energies are the forces of imagination through which a human being produces objects. Thus, he lives in fixed social structures and norms, and his life expresses itself according to them.

Within cause and effect the fictive 'inside' and the fictive 'outside' are reflected. It is actually attachments which are reflected, attachments arising on the relative plane which are sensed and understood as real. What is relative exists within Totality. Indeed, it only exists because its existence is derived from Totality.

The effects of the external world on the internal person are truly unpredictable. Therefore, the awakening one retreats before the influences of the world are upon him, and abides in silence.

The space between one occurrence and the next is the space where a human being judges and evaluates the course of these movements in relation to other corresponding experiences. He considers the knowledge he has gained from his experiences and identifies with them. Indeed, they are *his* experiences and *his* knowledge.

Through these inner movements and processes the human being creates a vast amount of knowledge and bonds with it. He stores this knowledge in his brain and learns from what he knows.

Humans have the gift of being able to analyze what they know and develop it further, and this seems important for the world. Knowledge is constantly remembered and renewed, and sensed as real and true. With this gigantic arsenal of remembered information at his fingertips, the human being defines himself, his life, and the world.

Hardly has something come to an end when something new begins; this is how time passes. The constant shifting from happiness to unhappiness and from unhappiness to happiness is strenuous and exhausting. Thus, a human seeks something that is beyond what is subject to change, something which lies beyond the impermanent.

The feeling of experiencing happiness or unhappiness is bound to particular events, experiences, and objects. It is obvious, then, that happiness and unhappiness have their origin in 'I'-consciousness. To be deeply aware of this is called awakening.

Therefore: one who deeply penetrates, sees through and overcomes the origin of this fallacy. He enters the Great Silence and is content without any cause. Neither the intellect nor the brain nor consciousness can comprehend, understand, or know this unfounded, unaffected joy. One who returns from all conceived paths enters the unconceived, the Great Silence.

11.

The person who inwardly ceases to come and go arrives at no other place than there where he already was before he started to come and go. Along all his paths and his path of returning, Totality never changed; indeed, it was never disturbed or influenced in any way.

His travels were all movements which took place in what seemed like reality, but where, in reality, nothing ever really was. That which was always present had no knowledge of that game of ignorance.

The silent one is eternally impersonal, unfettered, and beyond things and objects. He has the capacity to penetrate the most faraway places, while abiding quietly where he is. His inner eye penetrates everything and perceives everything, though his physical eyes which adhere to the outer world remain closed all the while.

He doesn't need to satisfy the mind with understanding, for he knows without knowing. Penetration is the natural presence of silence; he therefore affects everything, without himself being effective!

What prospers through the senses is subject to impermanence, and maintains its life through dead ignorance. Thoughts become words and words become deeds. But the silent one lives *prior to* thoughts, words, and deeds, and he is aware of this. The essential lies before thoughts, words, and deeds; the ever-present, the Eternal, is eternally silent.

Events push a person along a path. The human being crosses over immense inner fields of emptiness without being aware that all events, as well as the sense of emptiness are, in reality, unreal and void.

By extinguishing the old hardened images of 'I', a bright, invisible gate opens into a subtle and sweet love that flows beyond the body and beyond forms and objects.

There is a gravity to the perceived and interpreted thought-images and mentally conceived ideas of physical forms and objects which one produces. These projections pull the soul down into the abyss of time.

The personal struggle, the restless effort and tragic strain of life rushes on with the entire movement of the world. These highly charged, scattered energies control and constrain human life.

Weary, clouded eyes look upon the mire of time. They stare into the space where raw forces of the 'I' become dull existence. Confused and unclear human beings live in and live out their own subjective misery in the fictitious isolated domain of 'I'.

And yet, in every beat of every heart there is also a liberating entreaty, a call to awaken arising from luminous, 'I'-less depths. When the heart awakens, it is able to hear the magical tone ringing from the Great Silence. A soothing bliss expands within and tenderly heals the soul.

The sheath of loneliness which is woven into time quietly disappears. Primitive instincts which had endowed the flesh fall away and dissolve.

An inconceivable radiant transformation overtakes the entire being and integrates it into the Great Silence. This radiance stills the earthly senses, and the bloated 'I' burns away in the internal divine fire.

Emerging from all external and internal entrapments, the awakening one is aware that, in Totality, nothing has ever occurred. The descent from the magnificent realm of non-activity into animate flesh never really happened.

The Unchangeable never became the changeable, the Immortal never the mortal, and the Formless never became form.

That which has no name has no reality for the thinking mind. What has a name has meaning for the intellect and is therefore understood and acknowledged as truly existing. What has no name is meaningless and unreal for the intellect.

Within time there is a beginning and an end to things. In this superimposed 'I am'-realm the idea of one's own life exists, along with the idea that there are also many other individuals who exist and are continually experienced.

What is the cause of this individual being existing in the world, and what is the cause of the world itself?

If those things produced by thought are dispelled, a person attains the deep insight that the world was, in fact, never created, and doesn't even exist, other than as a reflection in consciousness. With this awareness the myth of creation is demystified. The awakening one goes beyond the boundaries of thought and realizes Totality.

12.

The remembered has *never* penetrated this radiance: the Eternal. Pure love was never caught up in heartlessness. The directive force of the will, the functionality of the 'I', was never active, for the subjective processes guided by the will are carried out exclusively in time and space. Consequently, they take place outside of Totality, though they are not separate from Totality.

In this oceanic presence the most wonderful of all is that the magnificence which lies in all and everything that is, is the *one* nameless, boundless magnificence. In awareness of the boundless depths of eternal presence, the limitless Unborn is fully revealed.

Falsely understood externalities lead to the conceptual and illusory sense of being born into the world, and to the ever-thickening illusory acceptance of a predominant central being out of which the Infinite should unfold.

But that which should unfold as the Infinite sets limits for itself, and limitations arise. Internal boundaries are external war zones and battle fields. When internal worlds of the will are active, activities are destructive and egocentric. Tragically, the bright and silent heart has been driven from its home by the actions of the 'I'. To be separated from the Totality through egocentric acts is akin to a disturbance of the rhythms of the cosmos within the soul, a painful sense of being lost in the fleeting world.

In this way everyday life is covered by a personalized veil of mist. But whatever may happen or has happened, it happened outside of the *one* unchangeable reality. Things happen and things change, but you are always the same.

Caught up in the current of the fleeting world, human beings are thrust across the swamplands of suffering. Still, the wonderful divine source is never subjugated; the divine fire is never extinguished. Its white light lies dormant in all hearts; it never withdrew itself from anyone. The immensity of eternity is the Great Silence. The Great Silence never stirs the senses. It is unchangeable, ever-present. It is the divine source, the foundation of all being.

Amidst the fleeting exists the non-fleeting; in the midst of darkness there is light.

The mystery within the eternal core is the boundless and superb presence of the supra-personal power of love. It exists in absolute absence of an imaginary, personal 'I'.

As long as a person remains trapped in memories and lives from memories, he is not conscious of the unreality of the world. He therefore lives distant and disengaged from the true divine core.

13.

The desires which eat through the flesh like a raging fire instigate and sustain a darkening within the consciousness of human beings. Enslaving powers ensnare the soul and clasp it tightly in dark abysses. The soul is driven through the realm of death as if in a trance, half asleep, possessed by lustful thoughts, jealousy, and the thirst for power.

The primal tingling felt within the body, the desire to procreate, resides in humans just as it does in animals; it motivates our collective life on earth.

But the inner chamber of lust is cast open and purified as soon as the light of silence flows into the heart of human beings. This gentle glowing fire is able to open doors buried and long forgotten.

Here the light encounters gloomy spheres where dark clouds of thought hover, and suffering images appear like pus oozing out from old wounds.

Shameful feelings of bad conscience, of having sinned, accompanied by indistinguishable fears, move languidly, washing up from hidden worlds to the surface of being. The forces which the human being has mentally downloaded want to be lived out, and they compel the human being to action.

But indeed, the gentle glow of pure being overcomes all mental compulsions and all obsessive intentions. When they are touched by the liberating light, the deepest core within human beings recognize it and feel it intensely.

Due to this impulse of awakening an attempt is made to elevate crude earthly substance into the subtlety of the Divine, and fails. Why?

Willful effort is not appropriate. What is called for is the deep insight that everything which a person knows, understands, and experiences can never be *what he really is.* When this is realized, everything unreal falls away. To be conscious of this, no willful effort is necessary, no spiritual practice.

Mental processes should not be controlled or suppressed. If a person encounters the light of all lights, a deep self-surrender takes place in a completely natural way. Human beings are transformed and spiritualized through this contact. The 'I' withers, and wisdom comes to flower.

Humility and renunciation untainted by intention are essential. But renunciation does not mean to give up objects. Rather, it is the realized insight that the world as it appears and recedes in consciousness never truly existed.

What affects the body belongs to the body and is transitory. What is eternal is eternally untouched by all that belongs to the physical body, although the Eternal is its essential foundation.

When a human being awakens, the old voices of thought are quieted. The awakening one becomes more and more silent, and less and less smitten with the egocentric forces he had given life to, forces which made him want to hold tightly to the world, forces which made him sick. Gradually the old doors close and deep serenity settles in.

Looking back into the limited, the past appears like an obscure dream which a dreamer once dreamed. This is how the awakening one looks on at what he, in reality, *never* was.

14.

Non-doing bestowed normality; doing *nothing* was *never* suggested. Upon awakening, the old cravings dissolve on their own in a mysterious manner, and the soul basks in gentle non-doing. In this bath of light, ill seeds planted long ago are burned away.

That which lies *prior to* cumbersome thoughts and limited words is flawless Non-Being, the eternal Here-and-Now. In one's Here-and-Now-Being a person never had an experience and never went anywhere. Curious indeed, that the human being believes himself to be something he, in reality, never was.

The desire to find oneself in a spiritual sense has produced many ambiguities and misunderstandings. The confusion is ever-expanding, because what is searched for is packed into conceptual forms and ideas. This has also led to a subtle accumulation of strange concepts of power and assertions of authority.

Through the 'I', which is caged in rigid concepts, the '*Not*-I', true presence, is excluded.

'Not-I' does not allow itself to be explained or described, but nevertheless, 'Not-I' is exactly what the human being really is. 'Not-I' is *that which is* before *something became something.* 'Not-I' is here and now.

The gate to eternity is found in the deepest core of the spiritual heart and beyond the breathing form. The Immeasurable never had a place amongst things measured, and that which is free of a past can never be found in the past. Eternity was never a person and a person was never eternity.

Therefore, the human being is something completely different from what he thinks he is. When he sees this, he penetrates through the outer world that is reflecting in his consciousness, and recognizes himself.

Self-recognition is also called awakening. Self-recognition doesn't recognize the person who wants to recognize himself. His unreality is recognized.

15.

The bars which inhibit one from entering the mystery were never actually there. The mental workshop in the brain invented and forged all those barriers, all the conceptual ideas that the human being has of life and himself.

The spiritual place you would like to go is exactly the place you are now, in this moment. The one who wants to go there, and the place which one believes he is moving in or moving toward, do not really exist.

The inner sense of being barred off arises through the frozen idea of being an individual who autonomously exists and functions. A path for an individual soul with a body has never existed, for what is imbued with soul is universal and not individual.

Just as a dewdrop evaporates quickly as it meets the light of the sun, the 'I-idea' of being something particular or someone special vanishes in awakening.

When the earthly cloak of the awakening one is permeated with the delicate radiance of silence, he becomes transparent and is transformed back into gentle illumination itself. All things polarizing and dualistic are dissolved; they never truly existed.

Yesterday and tomorrow are pervaded with grief, uncertainty, and monotony, but also with stimulating, inspiring, and exhilarating moments as well.

The burden of narrow thinking weighs heavily on the hours moving by, dulling the glimmering eye of awakening. Everything which the human being believes he possesses – including his body – will, in a fraction of a moment, dissolve into nothing. Everything which he believes is his and calls his own is merely a game of thoughts, and such thoughts arise from the illusion of 'I am'.

In confused souls the divine masterly powers have withdrawn to hidden worlds, but they have not disappeared. They wait to be wakened and discovered.

The soul suffers under the sense that there is no way out of this world, and from its arduous journey through the narrow realms of life and death. Decorative personal concepts have produced life agendas filled with hope, and with countless enchanting desires and expectations.

The active forces of the will produce all desires, all hopes, and expectations, and at the same time govern their own creations, the personal, self-produced concepts and objects of desire. In this way a tragic self-entanglement in an illusory sense of being occurs.

Force of will is only another name for the 'I'. Alas, the urgency of a life full of desires and hopes can never be completely assimilated and satisfied. A feeling of dissatisfaction remains, or surfaces soon after one thinks it is gone, because the one who wants, the one who wants more, remains active.

With astounding perseverance the 'I' staunchly busies itself with seeking happiness and satisfaction in fleeting objects and bodies.

In awakening, one becomes aware that objects and the body are comprised only of thoughts, and that the place where those thoughts arise is 'I am'.

Desires, hopes, and expectations dissolve in this awareness, and a person becomes content without any cause.

To see through the ephemeral structure of the being and to overcome it brings a great sobriety into life, which also prompts a deep healing.

The return to having no desires occurs when the human being awakens. The one who hoped and wanted is put into proper perspective and liberated.

An unpleasant emptiness inserts itself temporarily, because the 'I' has lost its playground and marketplace. Then, boundless silence expands.

16.

The old 'I' continually attempts to reconquer his territory; but no, the well-trodden paths which lead back have all vanished. Going back is no longer possible. That which would like to go back had never really existed. The 'I' is frightened of the unknown. The 'I' fears the 'Not-I'.

'I' would like to remain in what is recognizable and familiar, and when the dissolution of the 'I' begins, the 'I' suffers from severe symptoms of withdrawal and feels pain. 'I', which appeared temporarily in time and space and had identified itself, experiences its own death.

It requires time and patience before a drug abuser is healed from his addiction and is in no danger of relapse. It is the same for 'I'-addiction, the disease of the 'I' with its countless habits and confused ideas.

The volatile world was purged from the senses of the awakening one, and he has finally returned to his divine, borderless homeland.

The 'I', this peculiar dense shadow, was the strongpoint of the formed personal being. 'I' haughtily demanded its place in order to mark out its territory. This individualistic manner of being resembles a permanent solar eclipse. It is like a blind wanderer trudging through an unknown labyrinth.

But what is near was never far, and behind the night the sun was always shining.

The exile from eternity never occurred; the luminous eye that gazes backwards sees this clearly.

Words are bound to the finite, wordlessness to silence. No knower has ever been able to know the Great Silence, and no thinker was ever able to penetrate it.

What touches nothing remains untouched and is always pure. And so it is with the Great Silence. Silence is neither you nor I nor anyone else.

For one who has entered this silence, the alluring forces of the world are no longer able to pull him down. The awakening one has completely overcome the earth's gravity and everything which divides.

The awakening one has left that which was born on the earth behind him. He has departed from what seemed to be, and entered eternal being. He is the reality behind the universe that can be seen and experienced with the senses.

Just as a balloon filled with air bursts when touched by a sharp object, the entire fantasy world produced by thought bursts when it is touched by the superior powers of the Great Silence.

The ghost-like idea of an individual life was never more than a dream, never more than fleeting cosmic foam floating by. Self-discovery has brought it to the surface.

The space where the flesh is at home is the place where the dull weight of the world has been produced through thought. From image to image, from scene to scene, the personified being hurries through its realm, driven by burning passions which provide nothing but more suffering. Again and again the vulnerable creature is frustrated and distressed.

But there is an internal divine power which guides and protects the human being in difficult moments of his life, allowing him insight and making him aware of the existence beyond his experience.

The question is: does a person have ears to hear these subtle counsels and awakening whispers? Does he have eyes to see deeply and recognize within?

The venue that is externally visible is finite and limited, but beyond the stage and beyond the actors lies the Great Silence, the true home of the awakening one. This home is so near that even a slight breeze carries it far away.

The internalized is the externalized, and the externalized is the internalized; they condition each other. These dichotomies never stir the Great Silence, for this condition of being exists solely due to the delusion of 'I am'.

One who attempts to approach the Great Silence fails. And one who would like to have it fails as well. Magnificently cultivated words and thoughts would like to grasp the eternal light, but their vain efforts are futile. The individual's network of thought-energies is of material nature, and it cannot go beyond its own limitations.

As long as a human being busies himself with acquisition and rejection, he remains trapped within the limitations of his 'I'-domain.

Just as shadows can never become the sun, limited thoughts can never become eternal presence. The Eternal is the gentle light of silence, the great mystery, the force beyond perceptible silence.

The shadowless depths of eternal presence are the home of the awakening one. He drinks from the inexhaustible source, and is one with the power which moves the stars. The rays of the Spirit shine through and illuminate each molecule, each cell of the awakening one's body – he is the eternal Here-and-Now.

The heart of the awakening one resembles an everlasting smile, and affirms the presence of a supra-personal, flourishing beauty. A never-ending transformation of form takes place, an inconceivable glorious alchemical process completes what is incomplete. Pure divine light becomes pure divine energy.

To be born or to die were never the goal, and neither was identification with the transitory. The descent into endless efforts and repetitions tires the soul, and striving to circumvent these energetic forces only serves to strengthen concepts.

To put an end to incessantly returning stories seems to be a spiritual objective and distant goal of the ego. Thoughts go to work in search of a means and opportunity to achieve this distant goal. But such old compulsive stories don't allow themselves to be driven out or shaken off so easily. This is because they are also produced from thought-energies and held together by them.

Being, without events or experiences, cannot be produced. Only the penetration of the functioning 'I' guides one over the borders of creation and into radiant 'Not-I'.

All efforts and activities are aroused by the idea of 'I am'.

Deeply aware that the superimposed personality and the world in which he lives is nothing but a concept; so it is with the awakening one. Insight ignites a colossal inner explosion, a big bang which moves through the entire universe. That which was nothing more than 'I am' is gone once and for all.

The rigidly outlined dominion of the 'I' knows highs and lows. 'I' experiences itself in its narrowly constructed domain. The 'I'-commander rules over the conquered, but the chilled plane of material life where everything is constantly liquefying and solidifying makes life difficult for 'I am'.

What constantly shifts can provide human beings neither joy nor satisfaction nor security nor stability. Therefore, 'I am' fears the liquefying of his domain more than anything else; the loss of power and control.

'I am' cries for help and prays to God. He should stop this liquefying, and through his grace he should promote and glorify 'I am'.

Yes, *"May Your kingdom come,"* but please,

just as 'I am' imagines and wants it to be! Oh, how incredibly corrupt this 'I' truly is! The time-conditioned wants to make a deal with the Eternal, and through its cleverness, outwit the Divine.

The 'I' wants to employ the Divine as its instrument and use it to maintain itself. In this way it hopes it can ensure its own survival.

Material is characterized by the 'I', and the 'I' is characterized by material. These old hollowed-out ideas of God are never capable of touching or activating God. 'I' moves space and time, God moves nothing. Through spiritual cleverness human beings try to redeem themselves from their confinement. With myriad practices and holy hymns, they hope to become 'Not-I'.

Through haphazard knowledge all possibilities and strategies are exploited. Human beings want to enter this 'other', this timeless Promised Land, this wonderland where 'I am' can live on.

The false paths of the 'I' are convoluted and extend far and wide. The flustered forces of the ego forage through the mire of things past, rummaging in the chamber of death. The 'I' wants to plan and influence; it wants power in heaven just as it had on earth.

'I' wants to be recognized and acknowledged in all its splendor, and wants to display its powerful knowledge for all to see. And 'I' wants to measure itself with other 'I's.

Oh, what glorious spiritual competitions have been staged by the 'I', for the sole purposes of positioning and puffing up the 'I'.

Wisdom is not at home in this truly inscrutable game. The sovereign, omnipresent, divine force never allows itself to be regulated or restricted through such childish behavior.

17.

The freshly awakened soul is emancipated from it voracious seeking. It has left all its learned ways and information behind. The awakening one has seen through thought and the importance assigned to thought's inventions. He has exposed the relative insignificance of mental movements in the brain.

The awareness of the awakening one releases the cerebral clinging to the earth and the body-form.

Totality cannot be understood or grasped mentally or intellectually. Only direct intuitive awareness is ultimately capable of penetrating the world and the body; only direct intuitive awareness can realize Totality.

Therefore, the awakening one lives in total acceptance and harmony with all that is. He accepts everything that happens or doesn't happen in his life; everything beautiful, but also all difficult experiences and situations. He accepts them completely.

He has recognized that the entire force of cosmic being is exactly that which he is and what he experiences in Here-and-Now. Thus, all that he experiences on the relative plane is exactly that which was prearranged for him.

There is absolutely nothing which could take place separate from authentic presence. Therefore, all that happens, no matter what it may be, is immediate, flawless, and arranged perfectly!

18.

When vagrant unruly thoughts become still, that which lies behind thoughts is realized.

The *one* was never the 'other'; the disastrous 'I'-movements in the brain were never more than a faint flickering, a blur appearing in consciousness. The Great Silence never moved and was never abandoned.

In natural silent awareness, magnificent universal grace is revealed in fullness. It is the universal heart, the universal presence of the awakening one.

The foundation which could allow transitory existence to thrive has never really existed. The dimensionless spiritual heart was never actually bound to the relative circumstances of time: the immaculate gown of universal love has never touched the ephemeral world.

Life never ended in death; something or someone was never born or reborn. Eternal presence in all its immensity flows abundantly with the joy and beauty that reside within it. The awakening one, who lives detached from things and objects and is entirely free of intention, is this universal joy and beauty itself.

No conflict and no contradiction arise between the outer form and the vastness of the Timeless. True love never identifies.

The human being conditioned by time and space is led by his thinking into endless ambiguities. From them the idea arises that he could wed thoughts founded in the fleeting world with the Immortal. In pure awareness, all contradictions and concepts are seen through and nullified. Their irrelevance has been recognized, and the heart is set free.

Through complete acceptance of life in Here-and-Now, everything flows together within the awakening one, and flows back into Totality.

Complete acceptance does not mean that there is a person who accepts something outside or separate from himself. Complete acceptance is the awareness of complete Here-and-Now. Cosmic processes are not separate from Here-and-Now. What happens is not individual; it is always cosmic. The awakening one sees and experiences it in this way.

If one looks deeply, one sees that all that happens to the individual is embedded in cosmic processes. For it is this unity, this inseparable universal power itself, which allows all manifestations and experiences to occur. The physical form is a natural expression of this unified power. The actual conflict arises through identification of the inner life with the outer world. Awakening enables a dissolution and detachment from what was held on to, what was identified; freedom from the imagined 'I' and imagined 'others'.

19.

An abundant overflow of fabulous light force streams through the physical body of the awakening one, stimulating and transforming the cells. Through this, his true humanity and subtle divinity is revealed.

The majesty of non-ephemeral silence cannot be explained in human language, because it does not originate in muted material. Silence is not something, is not an object, and doesn't allow itself to be construed or objectified. Only that which is transitory, which is, from the perspective of eternal Here-and-Now, *not* true, can be objectified, understood, and explained.

The ever-widening earthly expanses from which day and night manifest are the home of the flesh. Heaven and earth are shrouded in death, for they dissipate again with everything that exists between them and through them.

This is not a tragedy. It simply shows the course of time in which 'I am' vibrates. Time is like a fleeting shadow, or like the reflection of a timeless, shadowless truth.

That which has been drawn together by natural forces will also be dispersed again. It is a cosmic movement in the finite, which allows itself to be objectified within the Infinite. Form becomes formless; the dense becomes liquefied, and the liquefied becomes gaseous.

But that which is aware has never touched the seen, never identified it nor become engaged with it. The finite can never elevate itself to the Infinite, and the Infinite never descends into the finite.

Polarities exist within the world of time and space. In the timeless awareness of the awakening one, they are abolished. Rational concepts are never capable of negating or superseding polar opposition, because rationality itself is conceptual.

One who awakens is aware that the present exists solely in the imagination, and that a sense of time is purely mental, since it is based on the concepts of a yesterday, a today, and a tomorrow.

The thinking mind doubts and despairs, is hopeful and hopeless. These characteristics belong to the viscous 'I'-world, which pours out of the brains of all human beings like a giant river. The invisible source from which the ideas of past, present and future arise is found in the brain. To penetrate the meaninglessness of these movements originating in the brain is called awakening.

20.

In the center which is found at no fixed place, there is the most delightful treasure, an inner wealth which was never seen or experienced in the daylight or at night. But the thought 'I am' also flickers in the middle, and from this thought the subjective world arises.

Nevertheless, the true center never became the world and the world never the center, because the center is not a place: the center is *everything* and *nothing!*

One who awakens in the center is not between two things. He is that which governs everywhere, without being something specific. The awakening one governs over everything without being a governor or commander. One who is in the center is not an 'I', not a person, and not a body, for person and body are nothing more than thoughts born of 'I am'.

The current that flows through everything is not separate from what is flowed through. Everything which is, is *One*. Although the One appears as two in its physical form of expression, there is only the One, the flourishing, omnipresent, all-encompassing center!

Through its flourishing, a sense arises within the Unborn of being born. Within the Unformed, a sense of existing as a form arises. The awakening one sees through this superficial illusion. As he awakens, he shakes off what duality generates and goes beyond this inner boundary. The awakening one sees the world as a drifting shadow; indeed, he has overcome the world. *He is that which exists before the world.* Those shadows are nothing but an overlay of ignorance; the awakening one is shadowless Totality.

The awakening one has no characteristics and never binds himself to the troublesome forces of the 'I' and its creations. Creations and places in the fleeting world were never the home of the awakening one.

21.

Subjective activism of the 'I' means adaptation to a permanently changing world within a narrowly defined social and cultural framework. This is truly no easy endeavor.

The idealized concepts of life that human beings have, with their expectations, demands and desires, are never entirely fulfilled and satisfied. This is because: first, things happen differently; and second, things happen differently than one thinks and hopes they will.

The yearning depths which are buried in the personality will never really be completely gratified. These burning desires and longings reside beyond the periphery of true being. They are nothing other than ego-movements, and are therefore hollow and void of substance. They are like thick gray smoke that lingers and only very slowly dissipates.

One who chases after his own thoughts is confused, and is not able to recognize that reality lies beyond thoughts.

The sensitive awakening heart longs for something unknown, for something beyond transitory objects. He yearns for liberation from the old accustomed ways and familiar forces of habit, to be emancipated from the ceaselessly repeating stories and the imaginary sense of time that goes along with them.

The awakening human being senses intuitively that something inconceivable, something enormous is the mainstay of his heart. He steers his gaze within, towards this divine power, and hopes to cross the invisible bridge leading from bondage to boundlessness. But that invisible stairway leading up to heaven doesn't exist.

Because a human being wants to be something important, special, something supernatural, he loses sight of the splendid simplicity of his actual presence.

When consciousness becomes dense, awareness falls asleep and becomes dull material. The divine luster becomes listless, the Eternal becomes temporal, and universal being becomes individual. The elimination of this dullness happens through the elimination of the idea of being someone special or wanting to become someone special.

A 'someone' is an object, and because an object exists solely as a transitory perception, the perceived is, in the deepest sense, unreal. To recognize this is called awakening. Awakening is the lack of the unreal. One who clings to the unreal is truly unwell.

22.

Reality – the Great Silence – is far beyond this mask-like world. A 'someone' or an object has never entered into this original radiance.

In the coarseness of personalized existence, in the tedious, tiresome struggle of life, a turning point arrives unexpectedly. A surprising divine ray penetrates into the heart of a person. A warm, motherly, universal power touches and awakens the one who is ready.

This sweet, subtle force of light arouses a tender feeling within the heart of a person and begins to gently transform him. The great turnaround is underway, and gradually the overlay of the unreal is dissolved.

In pure light-consciousness, in the center, the awakening one becomes aware of the Most Supreme. Through this divine radiance the body is transformed by a supernatural power; a human being is consolidated into the center. The depths of ignorance melt away almost unnoticed. This curative touch imparts a silent joy into life. A mysterious and truly monumental task is accomplished. The ambition to be and to become fades away.

Something luminous and majestic which wants to be realized shines like a thousand suns at the edge of human consciousness. This glory imbues the heart of the awakening one like a gentle celestial breeze. This glory is clearly perceptible for the pure heart, though it is absolutely incomprehensible and unimaginable for the thinking mind.

A human being would like to possess this glory for himself, and through his possessing desire he is drawn into a vortex which pulls him away from this radiant glory with rapid force. He was unable to understand the secret of allowing things to mature.

No cooperation exists between wanting and eternity. The tightly filled chests of desires for the inseparable truth are the product of dull mental forces and projections. Forces of desire attract all subjectively generated images of the inseparable reality to themselves, condense them, and attempt to possess and govern over them.

Desiring itself constructs the restrictive storerooms of the 'I'. Eternity cannot be something that one wants or could achieve at some point in the future. Awakening is here and now, but an awakening one doesn't actually exist.

The world comes and goes and can be destroyed. But since this world, in reality, doesn't even exist, it cannot really be destroyed. Therefore, the true human being abides in the center; he is universal, indestructible Here-and-Now.

23.

The surrounding environment of a person is the product of his passionate desires and concepts. They are reflections which cast a veil over what a human being really is. The road of destiny begins at this outer margin of consciousness. It is the place where cause and effect come together and are set in motion.

Strange; never has a person set one foot down on this road of destiny, and yet most people are convinced that their path of life is true and real.

The seer is the actual origin of the body; what is seen is the body itself. The one seeing is the cause; what is seen and interpreted are the effects. Without a perceiver there is nothing perceived; for this reason the world and the body are merely perceptions and subjective interpretations of the one perceiving.

Indeed, Reality abides *prior to* the seer and the seen, and *prior to* the one who experiences and what is experienced. Therefore, in Reality there is no destiny nor a dissolution of destiny; no path and no goal.

The sense of being sequestered in a sensual, gaily colored life happens entirely on its own.

Familiar habits install themselves and multiply in mental consciousness, where they become memories and characteristics.

Gazing out at nature becomes appealing and hypnotizing, because nature is the expression of the same consciousness as the one observing it. Nowhere is there separation, everything is *one!*

A universal entity witnesses the one observing and through him the observed nature. This universal entity is pure awareness. The awakening one *is* this awareness itself.

There is no world outside of consciousness, no nature and no body, because nature, the body, and the world are nothing other than consciousness. Spirit, however, lies beyond consciousness. Spirit is like the sun. Consciousness and the phenomena which reflect themselves in consciousness are revealed and become visible in Spirit's light.

Consciousness, the world, nature, and all apparent phenomena rest in Spirit. Spirit is that which a human being *really is.* Everything which manifests is spiritual, though Spirit itself is not. Because Spirit is un-manifested, formless and limitless, the awakening human being is also the Non-manifested, the Formless, and the Limitless.

The worlds of frequencies where the 'I' exists in space and time are located outside of Non-Being, outside of the Great Silence. In reality, the human being is that which precedes any manifestation.

Gods and paradises reside in consciousness, but Spirit is the Great Silence, the Eternal; it is the sweetness, the wonder, and the infinitely gentle. This all-encompassing, bodiless and formless radiance constitutes the deepest inner truth of human beings.

The spiritual feeling within the heart is the source of abundant, care-free joy, and provides a deep peace which never regresses. One who awakens no longer descends into meaningless mental movements, and no longer gets carried away by the commotion of a subjective, illusory life.

Living in a body in bodiless bliss, the awakening one abides here and now in the Great Silence. His is surrounded by noise caused by human beings, but the noise doesn't penetrate, doesn't affect him. Certainly, the greatest producer of noise is the 'I'.

The exaggeration of truth as well as the exaggeration of untruth lead to many misunderstandings, disagreements, and heartlessness. For this reason the awakening one is and remains silent – in the center. He is deeply aware of the power of thoughts and words.

Huge effects originate in small causes, and one who becomes involved with them remains bound to externalities.

Subjective superimpositions lead to false subjective images and concepts. Thus, the silent one remains silent; he gives no further life to things. He is free of characteristics and formalities, and aware that all mental exertions are in vain. What is eternal cannot be observed and understood, for every urge to action has its source in the superimposed, ephemeral idea of 'I am'.

Insight induces a return, and returning dissolves the old strands of identification. All strivings of the ego collapse and cease to be active.

24.

The questions of what is right and what is wrong arise in the external world. Internal retreat breaks through this shadowed, insecure illusion. Retreat happens directly, when the dream, the theater of life is discerned. Where the sun shines, no night appears, and where no 'no' appears, no 'yes' appears.

The internal dissolution of externalities enables a unification with the Boundless; the Boundless is the Great Silence. That which is subject to death is never able to encounter what is immortal, and the superficial is never able to recognize the fundamental, beginningless source.

The earthly, mortal mind thinks it can cooperate with the Immortal, and hopes in this way to transform the bitter past into a flourishing future. But resistance in the high-strung mind is powerful, and the primary result is inevitable: confusion.

The hopes and ideas of one's own personal world and its formal life-style are built out of mental, impermanent material. They inevitably cling and remain affixed to the space they originate in.

As long as the old desires are not dissolved, the dull force of their assertions are active. The resulting impermanent condition leads to the inner crypt of death. A human being is entangled in forces of dissatisfaction, doubt, and disappointment, though he ceaselessly strives to free himself from their grasp.

Be aware: the realm of light in the deepest internal heart has never left a human being, even when he feels he is cut off from all universal goodness. The most internal depths, the Eternal, has no connection to external causes and their effects. It cannot be approached through apparent facts or truths. Those internal depths are the Great Silence.

25.

There is no mathematical formula for transcendence. And yet the heartbeat of eternity, without palpitating, is present in all hearts. One who can sense this subtle heartbeat is truly alive; one who doesn't feel it is numb. Yet, there is no numbness that cannot be revived.

Just as ice melts under the sun, numbness softens when it nears universal love.

Something deeper, a divine power, connects all of nature. A universal live-giving current flows through and permeates the world and all living beings. One who awakens becomes one with this divine current, which doesn't bring the awakening one anywhere, for there is no beginning where it originates, and no goal where it could flow towards.

The truth of a human being *is* this divine current, free of identity and identification, free of space and time.

A human being should be aware of his innate divinity – the deepest inner core: the Untouchable, the Inseparable, the formless void.

When the awakening one enters his original home, he is suffused with immeasurable beauty and tenderness. In astonishment and wonder, he is aware that, in reality, he was never anything other than beauty and tenderness, and that he never knew death.

26.

Compassion is limitless and immeasurable, and never fixed to one person or one group of living beings. Compassion knows no separation, and still the awakening one carries the burden of the world. He carries the burden of the world, but it is as light as a feather and never weighs him down.

The compassion of the awakening one offers shelter to all; yet, no one and nothing can hide in this universal shelter.

Everything earthly and transitory falls away from the human being who integrates in eternity. Without doing, he unites with eternal presence and becomes that which he united with.

The awakening one doesn't strive to learn new things anymore, and doesn't busy himself unnecessarily, while the unawakened one is constantly striving to learn and be active.

The one striving wants to prove something to himself and others. The one who no longer strives has nothing to prove to himself or others, for the old, superfluous, illusory necessities have fallen away.

The awakening one has overcome all lethargy. In his *non*-striving and *non*-learning, he is the strongest power in the world. He is power *without* strength.

One who discovers his internal depths does not concern himself with externalities, but nothing external is ignored. All things are considered with diligent care.

One who is primarily concerned with the external world ignores his inner depths and is not aware of his boundless presence. The one who lives in the outer world without inner depth is like a living dead man, and he causes great damage in the outer world.

The visible world was never created, and yet it moves. The human being who is aware of the consciousness within which everything resides is empty, is universal - Totality.

One who forgets what he really is, is primarily concerned with what he *really is not*.

27.

The awakening one is silent and selfless. He transforms within, but goes nowhere. He is unseen, yet he is everywhere; a pure light for everyone and everything.

One who flows knows no stagnation. One without stagnation flows everywhere.

The awakening one is the great water that never dampens others. Luminous throughout the entire universe, he is the revelation of divine grace. He is the consummated, the coalescence of heaven and earth; he is the great equilibrium between the visible and the invisible.

One who doesn't act is available to the universe and contributes in abundance.

One who unifies enters the Great Order and ends all disorder. One who unifies overcomes his lack of direction and experiences direction.

In awareness of unification the awakening one recognizes that he is *in* the world but *not of* the world.

One who unifies flows back into the Boundless, the Unformed; into that which was never born and never dies.

The human being who seeks the meaning of life in words remains trapped in the specified, categorized world of words. To seek the truth in the meaning of words is meaningless. Eternity is not to be found in the word 'eternity'.

What flows from words belongs to worldly existence, while deep wordless silence belongs to Non-Being. What is inseparable does not let itself be clothed in words.

Beyond the world of words, deep silence reigns. This is the home of the mysterious light which shines without blinding. It is the home of the awakening one.

One who awakens discovers the wisdom *behind* the words. Not thinking, the meaningful is realized; not acting, what is right is done; not wandering, the way is known. This is the bearing of the awakening one's silent heart.

The breath of life leads to aging and the decay of the body.

Of what concern is this to the one who awakens? He was never the body, and his formless omnipresence was always present.

That the soul arrives from an invisible realm, and is now in a visible realm, and that later it will return to the invisible realm – this is merely an idea, an assumption which is hollow and unreal.

One who lives in the external world is self-absorbed and casts dark shadows on the world. Stumbling forward through life in ignorance and uncertainty produces massive suffering and enormous fear. Confined within the 'I'-being, this schoolyard is all that exists for the one who has turned away from the divine light.

This internal forgetting resembles a descent into the night. But the invisible golden umbilical cord was never severed from its origin. Even on the darkest night, a refined divine light glows within the veiled heart.

The condensed thoughts that produce the good and the bad generate complex and idiosyncratic conceptions and lifestyles. Such subjective schemes of life are the breeding grounds of thriving egotism and parasitic behavior. Without the 'I am'-concept there would be no breeding ground for an egocentric life.

The wickerwork of thought's creations is massive and complicated, and therefore erratic and unpredictable as well. The geographic landscapes projected by the 'I' are compiled within the brain as relevant destinations, and can therefore be experienced as a reflex outside the body.

The 'I' experiences itself and celebrates itself. In the process, it is not conscious that it itself is hollow and lacks true existence.

The experiencing object as well as the experienced object are inextricably linked to each other. They are one and the same, and both are unreal. The external world surges inwards, and the inner world surges outwards; this is how the mirror and its reflection function. How big and how thick the subjectively reflected world is, is unknown. Perhaps it is no thicker than the transparent wings of a dragonfly, and no heavier than a feather.

28.

The human sense of immortality is not yet the true Immortal. The mentally fabricated ideas and longings, the hopes for a grand heavenly union, are wishful dreams and remain so. The Immortal is not far away, is not a foreign world. It is the closest thing, the absolute Here-and-Now. But one who attempts to achieve Totality remains forever separated from it.

How heavy is the oppressive anxiety concerning one's own life, and how light is the encounter with one's own heart? How large is the gap between life and death, and how large is the gap between the conscious and the unconscious?

Such questions and uncertainties have never impeded the Great Silence. Never has anyone ever persevered through an agitated, disoriented world.

Meaning and meaninglessness and the aimless exploration of one's own ego-world are illnesses of the 'I', and not the Great Silence. The conditioned limits of what is apparent to the senses is not able to penetrate the immeasurable depths of the Limitless and Formless.

Everything which happens, happens only here and only now. Never was something outside or separate from Here-and-Now. And yet, although it is enormous universal energy, Here-and-Now is absolutely empty of events or deeds.

To expose the uselessness of the world, to unveil the futility of life and death ends the ancient struggle of having and losing, of wanting and achieving. Independence from having and losing imparts a superb equilibrium beyond the world of objects.

A human being is not an object that lives in the world, but rather the great equilibrium beyond the world. The world is composed of dust; the soul is not. The soul exists in the Totality; it is inseparable Totality.

Natural selflessness is free of wanting and not wanting, free of doing and non-doing.

29.

One who believes he has something attaches himself; one who believes he has lost something is full of fear. Therefore, the awakening one sees the uselessness of the world and never moves from the Great Silence. Effortlessly, water flows to the sea; effortlessly, the awakening one flows back in Totality. This flow is the secret, and not the arriving.

Where there is activity, there is also success and failure. Where there is emotional love, there is also heartlessness. Therefore, the awakening one doesn't move from silence, and is conscious of the uselessness of the world.

Silence never yields a sound; light never casts a shadow, and a shadow never emits light. One who is connected within smiles upon the veil of external things and abides in the Great Silence.

Life lives itself; death dies of itself. One who loves life and fears death lives in turmoil. One who is one with heaven and earth knows no beginning and no end. The detached one never arises and never fades away; he abides in the Great Silence.

The meaning does not lie in activity within the world; through non-activity, one overcomes the world. Still, non-doing does not mean doing nothing. One who is non-active is the most dynamic force in the world.

Obviously, the meaning of being cannot lie in the external, impermanent borders of the world, in the illusory images of a physical existence. Assumptions and supplements to these assumptions are what construct the external world; and if it is external, it is impermanent. Indeed, the external will never become the internal core, just as smoke will never become fire.

30.

Closed eyes are a symbol for the concealed; open eyes symbolize what is shown. Beyond both is the Great Silence. The one with eyes closed does not see the world. The one with open eyes sees the world. That which appears and disappears again is not the true presence of the awakening human being.

Things originate from of a mysterious power: this is the indigenous home of all the stars and all living beings, and the intelligence that determines their movements. Though changeless, everything changes and transforms through this mysterious power.

The human being flows along in this mysterious, limitless ocean; one with the entire sea of stars, one with all living beings. Thoughts flow through, feelings flow through; a human being is a flowing, pulsating, vibrating molecular system within Totality.

The essence of a human being is being human, and no one knows what being human really means. But one might 'dis-cover' it. Being human means more than mere thoughts, and more than the existence one has assumed and interpreted.

The mysterious power is an intelligent, creative force, and whatever appears and disappears within this mysterious power can never be separate from this power. Everything which is, is this one mysterious power itself.

Silent eternity, this immense spiritual power is essentially and exactly what a human being is. The splendid and boundless manifestation of the visible universe offers a home for the immeasurable spectrum of living beings on the earth. But the true spiritual home of living beings is not the transitory earth; it is the mysterious power of pure Spirit.

It seems that, through an unknown mechanism, what is hidden is revealed, and an unknown, mysterious intelligence abiding within oversees what is revealed.

The silence within the heart is this mysterious power, this eternity beyond time. So lives the awakening human being, imperishable within the perishable, fleshless in the flesh. He constitutes this boundless magnificence beyond thought and form.

The awakening one lives in awareness of this mysterious, divine, oceanic power; he flows in endless, invincible, boundless peace. He is the Great Silence itself.

The reflected image of his physical appearance in the world does not delude the awakening one any longer. In deep awareness of the mysterious power, he has 'dis-illusioned' himself. The transcendence of inner boundaries and entrance into the Boundless was effortless, for the presumed boundary never existed.

There was never a beginning and never an end; those shadowed images of thought were never real.

The sum of all knowledge dissolves in the current which flows into the mysterious, divine ocean. Still, nothing was carried into the Immeasurable, for what was left behind never really existed, other than as a temporary image in consciousness, as a perception of the impermanent within the impermanent.

The fleeting moments of a life on earth withdraw again. But they do not appear out of nothing, and do not return to nothing, for they are the unchanging mysterious power itself.

The awakening one is before all appearances and beyond all cosmic actions. In deep awareness, he has transcended the consciousness of the mind, and this transcendence has left him humble, uncomplicated, and compassionately clear.

The cosmic mystery of flowing out and flowing back is indication of an immeasurable, inconceivable, and indescribable magnificence, the true spiritual home of a human being!

*And so, thousands of years ago,
the human being set out on the long
and arduous path to eternity;
but he was already there,
before he set out on his path!*

If you would like to attend a gathering
with Master M
or if you have any other questions,
please contact Mark Albin at
organization@mariomantese.com
or refer to the website at
www.mariomantese.com

In Touch with a Universal Master

This unusual biography portrays the life and boundless spiritual workings of Master M through narratives of his very early students.

ISBN: 978-3-7699-0626-4
www.dreieichen.com

In the Land of Silence

This autobiographical novel depicts a seeker's fateful encounter with a spiritual master in the Himalayas; from his challenging initiation to his deep realization.

ISBN: 978-3-8423-9166-6
Publisher: www.bod.de/www.bod.ch

What You Really Are

Master M responds in 18 very clear and vibrant chapters to the deepest spiritual and philosophical questions of our time.

ISBN: 978-3-7322-0193-8
Publisher: www.bod.de/www.bod.ch

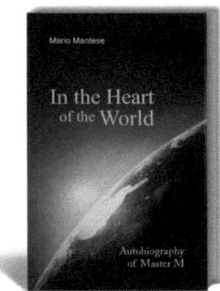

In the Heart of the World

This very personal autobiography offers a detailed and luminous description of Master M's journey to the core of the universe, and allows the reader to fathom the path of cosmic mastery.

ISBN: 978-3-7386-7267-1
Publisher: www.bod.de/www.bod.ch

Blessings – A Man of Miracles

This collection of twenty-one narratives from people who have known Mario Mantese – Master M – for many years, is a fascinating and insightful view into the life and work of a modern spiritual master. Over 200 of his clear, straightforward, and often humorous responses to spiritual and philosophical questions are included.

ISBN: 978-3-7386-8059-1
Publisher: www.bod.de/www.bod.ch